Original title:
Rootbound Reflections

Copyright © 2025 Creative Arts Management OÜ
All rights reserved.

Author: Arabella Whitmore
ISBN HARDBACK: 978-1-80581-857-1
ISBN PAPERBACK: 978-1-80581-384-2
ISBN EBOOK: 978-1-80581-857-1

## Shadows of Growth in Hidden Hollows

In a patch so snug and bright,
A flower tried to take its flight.
It stretched and yawned in morning glow,
But hit its head on a branch below.

A worm popped out, all muddy and sly,
"You're too ambitious, my friend, oh my!"
The flower chuckled, then gave a sway,
"Today I'll bloom—I'll find my way!"

A ladybug wearing a tiny hat,
Joined the banter with a cheerful chat.
"Why not dance instead of being stuck?
Let's embrace this earthy luck!"

So they twirled in shadow's fun,
In hidden hollows, the growth begun.
Life's a joke, a playful jest,
In nature's midst, they felt the best.

## Cracked Ground

On lonely earth, the cracks would talk,
They whispered tales while the sun would walk.
A stony face with a crooked grin,
"I love a drought—come on, let's begin!"

A cactus nearby, with its arms raised high,
Said, "I'm dry, but that's how I fly!"
It twirled in place, all prickled and proud,
As the cracked ground chuckled, out loud.

A grasshopper leaped with a silly bounce,
"Come on, ground—let's give it a flounce!"
They danced beneath the merciless sun,
Cracks and laughter—oh, wasn't it fun?

In the midst of heated, parched debates,
Life still sparkled, in odd little traits.
With jests and winks, they thrived all around,
The party was on—oh, cracked, silly ground!

## Unseen Beauty

Beneath the soil, where no one's peering,
A root's got dreams—it's boldly steering!
"I'm more than dirt; I'm quite profound!"
The little root whispered, making a sound.

A shovel passed, all shiny and new,
"Just wait until they see my view!"
But the root just giggled, with roots all a-tangle,
"Beauty's not seen; it's tucked like a mangle."

A worm with wisdom joined the spree,
"You've got the best seat—just wait and see!"
"Underground jokes? They're worth their weight,
Who knows what blooms before it's too late?"

As the world above pranced and preened,
The root just chuckled, feeling quite keen.
In unseen beauty, laughter took flight,
Joking with the earth, beneath the light.

# **Entwined Journeys of Time**

Two trees in a dance, oh what a sight,
Their branches twist, oh so tight.
They argue who's taller, who's the best,
While squirrels giggle, they're quite impressed.

With roots all tangled like a pair of shoes,
They share the gossip, the latest blues.
The sun peeks in, just to have a laugh,
As wind whispers secrets on their leafy path.

A leaf fell down, and then a fight,
Who dropped it first? Such silly plight.
They swear it's true, their tales they weave,
While the grass below just winks and leaves.

In sunlight's glow, they sip the breeze,
Planning their pranks on passing bees.
Together they stand, in time they find,
Entangled joys that are quite unconfined.

## The Silent Call of the Understory

In the hush of green, where shadows play,
Mushrooms giggle as they sway.
A beetle trips, on a leaf he slips,
And the ants chorus, 'Come join our quips!'

Brambles whisper, 'Is that you again?'
As rabbits munch, saying, 'Oh what pain!'
They riddle through thorns, with a cheeky grin,
And chuckle at tales of where they've been.

The ferns wave low, their fronds in view,
'What's the gossip? Come share, it's true!'
A slow snail shouts, 'I'm nearly there!'
While the world above is in a wild flare.

Under the boughs, oh such delight,
Creatures chat away in the soft moonlight.
In secret realms where laughter grows,
The understory hums, where chaos flows.

## Currents of the Quiet Veil

In stillness deep, where waters gleam,
Fish tell tales that make you beam.
With bubbles rising, they gossip low,
While turtles snap, 'Oh, don't you know?'

The reeds sway gently, they twist and twirl,
While frogs discuss the best whirl.
The dragonfly dances, a champion so spry,
Telling fish stories that just take the sky.

Under the calm, a world abuzz,
Nature sings softly, just because.
The ripples chuckle at sleepy snails,
Gliding along, with their slowest trails.

Yet in this hush, a mischief hides,
As the winds conspire and the current glides.
Laughter lingers in every flow,
As water wraps its tales below.

## Nature's Embrace of Forgotten Spaces

In corners where the wild things grow,
Old sneakers lie, wrapped in mossy glow.
Nature giggles, saying, 'Look what I found!'
As dandelions plot their next round!

Dusty ancient toys who've lost their charm,
Are cradled by ivy, a cozy farm.
They whisper stories of laughter and play,
As squirrels debate, 'Should we use them today?'

The sun peeks in, a curious light,
Illuminating treasures, oh what a sight!
Forgotten spaces, with secrets untold,
Where joy erupts and the brave hearts unfold.

Amidst the weeds, a party's in song,
Under the trees, they all feel they belong.
Nature's embrace, it's wild and free,
In forgotten spaces, where we all want to be.

## Buried Dreams in Darkened Corners

In a pot where dreams are tossed,
They whisper softly, counting the cost.
A shoe, a book, all jumbled, my dear,
Gardening's fun, but what's hidden here?

A sock, a toy, where did they go?
Under the leaves, with nowhere to grow.
Tangled roots play hide-and-seek,
Dreams suffocate; it's a little bleak.

Each plant smiles, but they all seem lost,
Is this how fun gardening is embossed?
In the corner, dust bunnies dance,
While buried dreams shuffle in a trance.

The snails are chuckling, taking a ride,
As I question this curious plant pride.
With laughter instead of garden glee,
I'll dig once more—just wait and see!

## The Weight of Undiscovered Paths

Footprints scattered on paths left unseen,
Who tied my shoes? It's all quite obscene.
I trip on thorns and giggle with glee,
Naturally I can't find a map, you see?

Adventure calls, but I'm caught up in jest,
Behind every bush lurks a new little pest.
Chasing the sunlight, I zigzag and spiral,
Each detour a laugh, a brand-new trial.

With every twist, my plans go awry,
Butterflies tease; I just can't comply.
A wobbly wheelbarrow and a rogue weed,
My garden's a circus; it's quite a breed!

So weigh the laughter, toss doubt aside,
Let's explore this path with whimsical pride.
For every mishap, there's joy to extract,
In this messy garden, my heart feels intact!

## Mycelium Murmurs in Twilight

In twilight's hush, mushrooms conspire,
Their whispers tickle, igniting desire.
A wiggly worm gives me a shout,
"Join the party! It's fun! No doubt!"

Under the soil, secrets abound,
With fungi gossiping all around.
Tickled by roots, they share tales of old,
Of lost garden gnomes and treasures untold.

Silly spores giggle, bouncing with ease,
As the twilight air hums with funky leaves.
I'll join the ruckus, let's dance under stars,
Who knew mycelium would give such bizarre bars?

In this earthy riddle, I twirl with delight,
Chasing fungi laughter, deep into the night.
With each little murmur, my heart starts to soar,
In this whimsical garden, who could want more?

## **Starlit Secrets Beneath the Ground**

Beneath the soil, where giggles take flight,
Stars are confiding in roots quiet and bright.
They chuckle and shimmer, what wisdom they share,
About plants with hats and worms that dance bare.

A carrot, a radish—deciding to scheme,
They plot in the dark, full of whimsical dreams.
"I'll be tall!" says one, "while you stay so round,"
Yet neither of them can see what's around.

The earthworms wiggle, just having a blast,
"Let's hide from the rain and hope it won't last!"
Each seedling chuckles as shadows drift past,
In starlit secrets, our laughter is cast.

As midnight tickles the garden's soft face,
Beneath our feet, joy finds its own space.
Fables from soil shall giggle and twirl,
In a symphony of light, let the night unfurl!

## **Twisted Memories of the Canopy**

In the branches, squirrels knick-knack,
Chasing dreams while I just sit back,
Sunlight giggles through the leaves,
As laughter whispers, 'Oh, just believe!'

A crow caws with a mocking tone,
While butterflies flaunt, in colors grown,
The air is heavy with memories spun,
In leafy arcs, we chase the sun.

By the trunk, a wise old tree,
Sways and chuckles, just like me,
Tales of pigeons playing charades,
In the forest's lighthearted parades.

As shadows stretch, and day goes dim,
Cherished seedlings pirouette on a whim,
Every twist, a laugh, a dance,
In this canopy of rooted romance.

## Dance of the Ancients Underground

Beneath the soil, the critters convene,
Worms in tuxedos, looking quite serene,
They shimmy and shake in earthy delight,
Hosting raves in the dead of night.

Mice tap their feet, like tiny drummers,
With stale cheese as the snack, oh what slumbers!
The roots twirl around, in whispers they scheme,
With potions of rainwater, they drink and dream.

Ants march by with a parade so grand,
Bringing tiny trumpets and a heavy band,
Who knew the underground had such flair?
With dirt as their dance floor, they'd jig without care!

As laughter echoes through the subterranean,
Even the rocks love a chorus in zany,
Dig deep enough, and you might just see,
How funny it is, to be wild and free.

## Depths of Longing in the Dark

In the darkness, shadows play tricks,
Waying mopey roots, with their comical licks,
The night is young, with giggles and snorts,
Even the weeds throw fanciful sports.

A toad croaks out a lullaby tune,
Quieting the crickets, they dance to the moon,
As darkness wraps all in a quirky embrace,
Every misstep finds its funny place.

Under the stars, the critters confess,
Longing for light—what a tangled mess!
But with each blink, a chuckle erupts,
Transforming the night, with hilarious hiccups.

So let's celebrate, even in gloom,
For mischief and laughter can flower and bloom,
Deeper may be the longing we claim,
But the joys in the dark, they always remain.

## The Weight of Forgotten Seasons

Oh, the leaves that once colored the sky,
Now crunch underfoot with a wistful sigh,
Can we talk about autumn's short reign?
It's like a fruitcake—endless and plain.

Winter fumes with its frost-bitten breath,
While snowmen argue about who'll meet death,
They topple and giggle, their hats blown askew,
Who knew cold could wear such a comical view?

Spring flirts with blossoms, a playful tease,
It throws pollen bombs with the lightest breeze,
Yet sneezes abound in a colorful spree,
Nature giggles, as joy runs free.

Summer arrives with its sunshine parade,
Wearing flip-flops, in sunblock charade,
But beneath all this laughter, watch seasons collide,
A tapestry woven with humor as guide.

**Enigma of the Earth's Embrace**

In a garden where the weeds play,
The daisies shout, 'We're here to stay!'
The carrots giggle, 'What a sight!'
While ants dance 'neath the moon's light.

Compost tales and wormy glee,
Potatoes root with such esprit.
The sunflowers wear the silliest hats,
While the broccoli teases the acrobatic bats.

With mud pies flung in playful arcs,
The cabbage reads its quirky quarks.
Earthworms shuffle in raucous delight,
While crickets chirp at the glorious night.

A dance of leaves in breezy flirt,
As nature sneezes, a muddy spurt.
With rhymes that tickle the soft earth's heart,
Life's a jest, but it's a clever art!

## **The Soil's Silent Serenade**

Underneath the buzzing bee,
The earth hums a lullaby spree.
Rocks roll over, cracking jokes,
While mushrooms ponder the world with pokes.

Ticklish roots in a soil soirée,
Turnip dreams take center play.
The peas chatter, the beans do brag,
As ladybugs zip in a zigzag.

Snails wear shells as funny hats,
And grasshoppers sing to their spats.
Windy whispers make everyone laugh,
As daisies recount their sun-filled path.

Frogs croak in a quirky tragedy,
While onions blush in mild majesty.
Down below, where giggles bloom,
The soil's secret is without gloom!

## Nature's Veil of Remembrance

The trees gossip in swirling spins,
Recalling when acorns were just twins.
With roots entwined like best friends' hands,
As flowers plot their colorful bands.

Breezes carry the tales of the past,
Where snails rejoice, never downcast.
Petunias laugh, 'We're fashion stars!'
While thorns and roses have their wars.

The clouds above whistle down tunes,
While rabbits think they're clumsy goons.
Dandelions boast in a golden cheer,
As memories grow beneath our sphere.

Fungi gather in huddled glee,
Sharing stories of shady spree.
With every rustle, a wink and a nod,
Nature's curtain pulls back, and it's oddly broad!

## The Depths of Unseen Resilience

In a puddle where frogs take a leap,
Worms whisper litanies, secrets to keep.
Rocks in the mud chuckle in jest,
While catnip sways in a furry fest.

The roots grumble, 'We're deeply set!'
While soil thinks, 'We're quite the bet.'
A dewdrop giggles, 'Watch me roll!'
As ladybugs play the comic role.

Potatoes hide in their underground maze,
While beetles strut in bold displays.
The grass grows tall, flexing its might,
Challenging clouds for a friendly fight.

Compost pals hold a nightly bash,
As stars twinkle, a dazzling flash.
In this world where silliness thrives,
Unseen strength is where fun drives!

## **Roots that Remember**

In the soil, we reminisce,
Worms waltz as we coalesce.
Forgotten dreams, they sprout and twine,
With each silly twist and vine.

Ants parade in a conga line,
While daisies tease, 'You're clearly mine.'
Old roots chuckle, 'What a throw!
Just watch us grow - quite a show!'

While daisies tease, 'You're clearly mine.'
Old roots chuckle, 'What a throw!
Just watch us grow - quite a show!'
Life underground is quite divine!

But gopher grins from his hideout,
Says, 'Up there? Always a drought!'
We giggle, clods our comfy beds,
In muddy dreams where fun never ends.

## Lament of the Underground

Down below, beneath the grass,
We giggle as the daisies pass.
A chickadee in a floppy hat,
Claims our soil is where it's at.

Rats chat with roots, oh what a sight,
While shovels bring a bit of fright.
They just want to dig and explore,
But we yell, 'No more, we implore!'

As moles groove to an unseen beat,
A party breaks with worms so sweet.
One bloated earthworm starts a dance,
And suddenly, we've lost our chance!

Yet as the world above turns bright,
We share tales in the twilight.
Growing old down beneath the fir,
We laugh, 'At least we can't deter!'

## Whispers from Below the Bark

Underneath where roots conspire,
We craft tales of leafy fire.
A wise old cricket hums each night,
His serenade is sheer delight.

The cover's tight, we plot and scheme,
'Beware of groomed lawns, they scream!'
As sunlight spills, we giggle loud,
'The surface world is such a crowd!'

A beetle joins with glittered shoes,
Swaying to the rhythm, he'll amuse.
We share our snacks of worms and dirt,
Crunchy bites, a tasty flirt!

From under bark, we jeer and cheer,
For nature's jest, we hold so dear.
What fun it is to twist and shout,
In tangled webs without a doubt!

**In the Clutches of the Clods**

Here beneath, we dance with pride,
Clods embrace us, a comfy ride.
But watch out for the shovel's gleam,
As we plot our underground dream.

Each lump and bump tells a tale,
Of gopher mischief, epic fail!
'Can't catch me!' cries the beetle bold,
As we weave through grasses uncontrolled.

And when the raindrops start to plop,
We bubble up, we twist and hop.
The roots sing songs of sweet refrain,
As muddy boots come down like rain!

But no one knows our secret cheer,
In clods we rest, without a fear.
With every squish, we burst with glee,
Just wait till spring, you'll soon see!

## Undercurrents of Silent Growth

In a pot too small for dreams,
A cactus learns to wear jeans.
Its spikes have quite the fashion sense,
But dances like a fence-hugging prince.

With roots that wiggle left and right,
It wonders if it's quite alright.
A wobbly jig on a Sunday morn,
And all the daisies sound the horn.

Careful now, don't trip a vine,
As they debate about the wine.
With laughter brewed beneath the ground,
They sip the nectar life has found.

A dandelion snickers near,
As worms conspire with a sly cheer.
Among these whispers, cheeky and spry,
They plot a garden party by and by.

## Whispering Pines

Pines crack jokes up in the breeze,
While squirrels take notes and sip on teas.
Their needles gossip, rustle and tease,
Who knew trees could aim to please?

Oh, what a hoot when the wind's just right,
They swap tall tales, giggles ignite.
"Did you see that owl? He wore a hat!"
They chuckle, hide from the silly cat.

In the shade of a trunk like a sturdy pole,
A funny old bear roars while on a roll.
He tells stories of bees with hats on their bums,
While puffing on dreams as laughter hums.

So gather around where the laughter flows,
And let the tiny creatures propose,
A soirée of giggles, amidst the roots,
Where the pines wear their best nature suits.

## Silent Echoes

In a garden of echoes, whispers disperse,
Where veggies gather and converse.
The carrots claim they're growing tall,
While peas just laugh, "We're short but we ball!"

A lettuce leaf critiquing the sun,
"Oh, it's too bright! This isn't fun!"
Tomatoes gossip out of sheer spite,
Plotting a heist for a pizza night.

But with each breeze that passes by,
They summon a breeze, hoping to fly.
"Let's make a salad! What's the hold?"
"Chill out, friends, let the dressing unfold!"

From roots to leaves, their chatter resumes,
In a patchwork of laughter, their friendship blooms.
With echoes that tickle and echoes that cheer,
They feast on joy, as the harvest draws near.

**Silt and Memory Intertwined**

In a puddle of mud, old tales reside,
Where memories squish and wiggle with pride.
The mud pies made by a child's hand,
Squeezed joy and laughter like grains of sand.

"Remember last summer? The splashes we made!
The frogs thought we were a messy parade!"
Silt giggles softly with tales to impart,
As they layer history like fine art.

A slimy old snail, wise in his ways,
Recalls wild chases on rainy days.
"Did the grass ever tickle your toes?"
With a wink, he whispers to the dirt below.

Time seems to pause in this muddy nest,
As memories wrap around hearts with zest.
Each squelch of feet tells a story anew,
Where laughter and silt blend the old with the true.

## **Tantrums of Earth and Light**

The sun threw a tantrum one fine day,
Shouting at clouds in a dramatic display.
"Step aside, you're blocking my shine!"
But raindrops giggle, "You'll be just fine!"

"Earth, don't pout! You're rich in mud,"
The daisies chime, "Let's don our flood!"
"Who knew this soil could dance so wild?
Come spin and twirl, you grumpy child!"

They painted their petals with golden hues,
Swirling and twirling in playful views.
And with each stomp, the ground laughed loud,
"A little storm makes you young, be proud!"

So the sun and clouds went hand in hand,
Creating colors across the land.
With laughter woven in rays of delight,
Even tantrums can bloom into light.

## **The Lilt of Buried Voices**

In the garden, secrets sprout,
Whispers of worms, oh what a clout!
Roots entangled, sharing jokes,
"Why did the carrot?"—punchlines evoke!

Raccoons tune in with mischief in mind,
Each burrowed laugh, beautifully blind.
Capers of compost, tales twist and twirl,
While daisies are giggling, giving a whirl!

Beneath the soil, the puns grow thick,
What's the funniest plant? An a-peel-ing trick!
Leaves sway and chuckle, a dance so spry,
As beetles roll by, with a glint in their eye!

So next time you dig, tune into delight,
For roots have a party, just out of sight!
They share their truths; it's quite a blast,
In the earthy embrace, good times never last!

## Bonds of Essence and Earth

In a patch of dirt, there's laughter loud,
With tomatoes frowning, they stand so proud.
Pumpkins grumble at the sun's hot rays,
"Why are we here?"—in a veggie maze!

The beet claims wisdom, an old, wise sage,
While peas crack jokes, filled with mirth on stage.
"Hey, what's the deal with roots so deep?"
"Don't bother us now, we're in too steep!"

Out in the garden, there's quite a riot,
Flowers trade gossip, oh what a diet!
"Did you hear what the garlic said?"
"Nothing, it's all in your head!"

With the sun as the DJ, what a scene,
Mixing up tunes for potatoes—so keen!
They laugh and they wiggle, till dusk arrives,
In the bonds of essence, silly joy thrives!

**Tides of Memory in the Soil**

Under the ground, old tales unfurl,
As kitchen scraps, make a dance and twirl.
"Remember that time?" the onions sigh,
"Why, oh why, did I have to cry?"

The carrots giggle at the turn of phrase,
While radishes blush in the sunlit haze.
"Life's a salad, cut it fine!"
In every twist of greens, a punchline!

Mulchy whispers of days long past,
In the burbles of soil, tales are cast.
"Why did the cucumber cross the way?"
"To become a pickle, oh what a day!"

In the tides of memory, so rich, so sweet,
Rooted in laughter, never admit defeat.
Digging up jokes, in the earth so grand,
Nature's humor, a glorious band!

## Intermediaries of Nature's Verse

In the shady glen, where shadows play,
Nuts exchange secrets in a nutty ballet.
"Nutty business!" they all chime in,
As squirrels join in, with a laugh and a spin!

In the dance of the breezes, whispers soar,
"Did you hear what the daisies swore?"
With roots intertwined, jokes flutter about,
As laughter erupts, making no doubt!

With every rustle, a punchline drops,
Grasses giggle, as nature hops.
"What's green and funny? A pea on the run!"
Chortles abound under the brightening sun!

And as dusk falls, the evening's a blast,
Nature's funny bone holds firm and fast.
So next time you wander to where trees immerse,
Just remember, they speak in nature's verse!

## In the Embrace of Earth

In the dirt, my thoughts reside,
Worms and bugs, my friends besides.
They wiggle, giggle, in their squishy dance,
While I ponder life's odd chance.

I try to stretch, but roots hold tight,
This cozy den feels just so right.
With muck and mire, I find my groove,
Unfurling slowly, trying to move.

Oh, who knew soil could be so grand?
I'm winning at life with a shovel in hand!
Digging deep in laughter's throne,
As garden gnomes stand schoolyard prone.

The sun's sweet rays tickle my face,
In this muddled world, I've found my place.
With every giggle, I just can't wait,
For the next big splash in my earthy fate.

## Memories in the Darkened Mud

In twilight's grasp, the earth does bloom,
With shadows dancing, chasing gloom.
The puddles sparkle, secrets keep,
While toads croak songs that make me leap!

Each splash brings memories of days gone by,
Of mud pies flinging, oh my, oh my!
I reminisce over clay-filled fun,
In the muddy chaos, we've surely won.

A rooster laughs with a crooked beak,
At my attempts to play hide and seek.
I slip and slide, a beautiful fall,
With nature's mirth, I ponder it all.

Stars twinkle down, still full of mirth,
In this muddy realm, I find my worth.
So here's a cheer for the muck and glee,
In the silliness of life, I am truly free!

## Where the Tendrils Confess

In winding paths, the vines entwine,
Whispered secrets in every line.
They stretch and stretch, oh, what a sight,
While squirrels giggle with pure delight.

Under leaves that rustle and sway,
Tendrils giggle at the games we play.
With every twist, a story unfolds,
Of critters bold and plans so bold.

The daisies nod, they know the jest,
As I attempt to grow with zest.
Who knew that roots could sense such charm,
Feeling safe in this natural farm?

So here's to the tendrils with tales to weave,
In every curl, they never leave.
With laughter sprouting from every hue,
In this green world, I feel brand new!

# Emblems of the Understory

In the shadows where mischief thrives,
The underbrush plays, where humor jives.
A skunk winks, not far from the ground,
As critters gather, joy abounds.

Amongst the ferns with playful might,
They share tall tales of the night.
With mushrooms giggling, and spores that glow,
Understory magic puts on quite a show.

A hedgehog tips his tiny hat,
Inviting a dance with a silly spat.
While lizards laugh in what seems like glee,
As they shimmy and shake, oh can't you see?

So here's to the joy in the leafy blend,
Where laughter echoes and friendships mend.
In this hidden world, wild and free,
I find the fun in life's great spree.

**Hushed Harmonies in the Ground**

In the garden, worms do dance,
Singing tunes of muddy chance.
Bugs plot with earth, a grand charade,
Sipping dew in nature's parade.

The daisies gossip, petals unfold,
While the carrots whisper secrets bold.
Oh, what a riot in the dirt,
As veggies shout, "We wear no shirt!"

Underneath the leafy skies,
Earthworms plot great garden lies.
With every squirm, they jest and roll,
While the radishes laugh, "We're on a roll!"

Beneath the surface, laughter brews,
As beetles play with muddy shoes.
The sun's warm rays, a spotlight's gleam,
On this wild and bloomin' dream.

## Secrets of the Granite Veil

Boulders grumble, tales they weave,
Of stubborn roots that won't believe.
In fractures deep, old rocks joke loud,
While mossy hats adorn each shroud.

Lichens laugh in colors bright,
Taking selfies in morning light.
"Let's pose, say 'cheese'!" the stones declare,
As boulders jostle, unaware.

Cracks in stone hold banquet feasts,
Where tiny critters are the beasts.
The granite chuckles, mighty yet small,
"Who's stronger now? Come one, come all!"

The wind carries whispers so sly,
As rocks reminisce under the sky.
In every crevice, stories spin,
Of laughter, life—let the fun begin!

## Beneath the Boughs of Reflection

Under branches, shadows play,
Squirrels frolic, come what may.
The oaks conspire, sharing a laugh,
"Who's stealing nuts? Do we have a half?"

A gentle breeze hums a merry tune,
While sleepy stones dream of a monsoon.
"Wake up, sleepyhead!" the roots exclaim,
As sleepy frogs hide from the fame.

The pond gurgles, stirring with jest,
As frogs wear crowns, they feel blessed.
"Let's leap to dance, we're quite the crew!"
With each splash, chaos ensues anew.

In stillness, the branches snicker sly,
While critters ponder, "How high can we fly?"
With laughter booming through the trees,
Nature's stage hosts a whimsical breeze.

## Soil-Stained Meditations

In the muck, where gnomes do dream,
They ponder life, or so it seems.
With trowels ready, they dig away,
Uncovering wisdom from yesterday.

A mushroom speaks, "I'm quite profound,
With roots and spores, I'm garden-bound!"
While daisies gossip, buds a-glow,
"Did you hear, old compost is the show!"

The bumblebees buzz with delight,
As flowers bloom, a colorful sight.
"Buzz off, my dear! This nectar's mine!"
Says the flower with a splash of shine.

Beneath the earth, so much to see,
Where laughter flows abundantly.
In soil-stained depths, life spins around,
In this merry mirth, true joy is found.

## Testing the Depths of Belonging

In the solitude of garden beds,
I ponder just how deep my roots spread.
They grip the soil, a firm embrace,
Yet whisper, 'Is this really my place?'

With weeds as neighbors, bold and loud,
They mock my growth, their tactics proud.
I chuckle at the awkward dance,
A flower's waltz, a clumsy chance.

Are these my kin that I surround?
Or just a sprout that's fallen down?
In sunlight bright or in shadow's gloom,
We share this space, my leafy room.

So I stand tall, in laughter's cheer,
Amongst the critters, far and near.
Belonging's odd, but what's the fuss?
We all just laugh, and that's enough!

## The Fresh Breath of Foundation

Beneath the surface, roots entwine,
They seek a path, a secret line.
In the tangle, a treasure trove,
Of lessons learned from earth's own grove.

With every wiggle, I try to breathe,
The stinky muck beneath my leaves.
Oh, the aromas! What a feat,
A foundation with a sense of beat.

I laugh at soil, it holds my fate,
But sometimes I think it's far too great.
To find the freshness in the muck,
While worms parade, 'How's your luck?'

Yet in this mess, I find delight,
A quirky step, a silly sight.
So here's my pledge, with roots so bold,
To cherish chaos, to stay uncontrolled!

## **Veins of Time**

Tick tock, I feel the pulse of time,
Each ring a tale, with rhythm and rhyme.
Circled whispers of sunlight's grace,
And stormy nights I can't efface.

In the silence, a joke unfolds,
As squirrels scurry, so brave and bold.
They chat of years with cynic's flair,
'Have you seen that root? We're all aware!'

My veins of time, a story spun,
From sprout to shade, oh what a run!
In laughter's glow, while shadows fade,
I jest, 'At least I'm not a spade!'

Time ticks on, a comedy show,
With silly plots that ebb and flow.
In leafy laughter, we thrive as one,
A rooty gang, oh what fun!

## Veins of Earth

Deep in the earth, my veins connect,
With giggles shared, they all expect.
To spread some joy, a ticklish touch,
Among the soil where we laugh so much.

The crusty shell, the roots' embrace,
A hug from nature, in our space.
And worms, the comedians of the room,
Wiggling wildly, yes, they bloom!

So here I sit among the grime,
Embracing chaos, one root at a time.
With leafy friends, we play our part,
The earth's own laughter, a work of art.

In all this mud, who needs a throne?
We'll crack up jokes in our earthy home.
For every vein brings joy and mirth,
A rollicking tale from our happy hearth!

## Unspoken Histories in the Mire

In muddy depths, secrets are kept,
Where laughter blooms and whispers crept.
The tales of worms, all intertwined,
With roots that tickle, joy defined.

What ancient trees would share if they could,
Of giggles echoing through the wood.
And in the mire, where all things blend,
A comedy fest where roots ascend!

Each clump of dirt holds a silly jest,
In the dance of spores, we're all blessed.
We swirl and laugh, a merry band,
Wiggling wildly in nature's hand.

So if you wander, take a glance,
At soil's embrace, it's quite the dance.
For in the mire, joy finds a way,
Laughter blooms bright, come join the play!

## Shadows Dancing with the Roots

In shadows deep where laughter grows,
A tree declared, "I'm just some prose!"
With tangled limbs, the roots will sway,
As squirrels giggle, come join the play.

The branches twist in silly ways,
Conversations bloom in leafy bays.
A dance of shadows, what a sight,
The critters twirl, oh, what delight!

With acorns dropped like silly seeds,
The laughter flows, just like the breeze.
A jester's hat atop a bough,
"Oh, how we party!" they all vow.

So here beneath the leafy cheer,
The roots keep talking, loud and clear.
In every dance, a quirky hoe,
Nature's jesters put on a show!

## Conversations with the Abyss

The abyss spoke back with a cheeky grin,
"Toss me a moose, let the fun begin!"
With echoes loud, they shared a jest,
"Why'd the tree fall? It couldn't rest!"

Amidst the darkness, giggles bounced,
A haunted squash, it still announced,
"Don't take life too seriously, you see,
A pumpkin's dream is to dance with glee!"

Down that void, a punchline flew,
"Why bring a towel? To save some dew!"
With every chuckle, the abyss would quake,
A cosmic joke, for heaven's sake!

So here we sit, both side by side,
Trading puns in a cosmic tide.
With laughter loud, we can't dismiss,
Even the dark deserves a bliss!

### **Whispers in the Gnarled Timber**

In gnarled timber, whispers play,
"Did you hear the tree's new way?"
It complained of knots and silly boughs,
"Why are there squirrels in my house?"

The branches creaked with tales untold,
Of acorn thieves, oh-so-bold.
"Did you see the owl in specs?
He's off to catch the memes of lex!"

The woodpecker tapped a rhythm fine,
"Let's have a jam, it's party time!"
With bark and laughter, they held tight,
A concert in the heart of night.

So listen close to timber's fate,
Their quirky tales do resonate.
In every groove, a giggle grows,
Even the trees have silly woes!

## Where Life Clings to Memory

In memories where laughter hides,
A garden grows with silly tides.
"Why'd the flower bring a broom?"
"To sweep away the winter gloom!"

Life clings tight to silly dreams,
Where daisies hum and sunlight beams.
"Is that a bee with fashion sense?
It's buzzing loud and quite intense!"

The roots hum softly, tales unwind,
"Let's party hard, we'll feel divine!"
Among the blooms, the whimsy flows,
As confetti petals dance like prose.

So cherish well those funny times,
Where memory winks and laughter chimes.
In every petal, stories bloom,
A garden where we chase the gloom!

## The Guided Descent

In a pot too small, I try to grow,
With leaves all tangled, it's quite the show.
The sun peeks in, a bright old friend,
But space, it seems, is what I must mend.

Digging deep down for the soil's worth,
My roots complain of a lack of girth.
I dance to the beat of a gardener's plan,
Yet my sprout's more like a wobbly span.

Bumping my head on the plastic rim,
I laugh with the bugs; who are we to skim?
Nature's a joker with a clever twist,
In search of escape, I play the list!

But alas, my plight is a tale to share,
Of how a little plant can show some flair.
With each little wiggle and flutter in place,
I find my joy in this crowded space.

## Quiet Ancestry of the Flora

In shadows, they whisper, the old sage trees,
Telling tall tales to a buzzing bee.
They laugh at their roots, all knotted and tight,
Hipster vines sipping on rays of light.

A daisy looks up with a cheeky grin,
Says, "I've got petals, where do I begin?"
The ferns roll their eyes, like, what's the fuss?
It's just a wild garden; come join the ruckus!

The daisies wink, as they lean to the right,
Belly-laughing through the warm summer night.
Each leaf's a letter in nature's own lore,
But all that they write is just begging for more.

And there in the corner, the moss gives a sigh,
"Dance with the roots, or at least give it a try!"
In the book of the unaffiliated bloom,
Each page is a party, come make room!

## Twined Footprints of Existence

In pots and in plots, our roots take a stroll,
Sometimes we trip, losing our goal.
We laugh at the mud on our leafy shoes,
"The dirtier the soles, the better the views!"

Around the old oaks, the critters parade,
We spin tales of life that never did fade.
The gopher with goggles gives us a wave,
"Now don't you forget, you're wild, not a slave!"

With worms in our hair, we dance with delight,
Each wiggle's a bob in the soft morning light.
We tangle our tales, in a jumble of cheer,
For life's just a giggle when friends gather here.

Each footprint a rhythm, we gently imprint,
In laughter, we flourish, no need for a hint.
So let the earth sing, let the seedlings hum,
We're twined in this journey, all stuck in the fun!

## Heartbeats Beneath the Surface

Under the soil, there's a party in play,
The radishes rave, while the carrots sway.
"Feel the vibrations!" the roots all shout,
As worms groove along, shaking all about.

"What's that?" asks the tulip, "a thump or a thud?"
"Chill out," says the clover, "it's just the mud!"
Each pulse tells a story, each wiggle's a score,
In the underground club, we're never a bore.

Mushrooms in capes are the bouncers tonight,
"Party hard, little sprouts, till the morning light!"
The daisies choreograph moves that they've learned,
While sprouts drumming deep keep the rhythm all turned.

So if you hear laughter coming from below,
It's just us, the seedlings, stealing the show.
In the core of the earth, our heartbeats unite,
In this secret ballet, we dance till it's bright.

## Tangled Whispers of the Earth

In the garden where I dwell,
The veggies converse, oh what a yell!
Carrots swear they're the best in town,
While potatoes just roll 'round, roll 'round.

The daisies giggle at the sun,
Telling secrets, having fun.
Roses blush, oh what a tease,
While weeds plot to bring them to their knees.

Earthworms wiggle in a party line,
While ants march past, feeling divine.
A cabbaged head holds court with jest,
Claiming to be nature's very best.

So dance, my dear plants, in sunlight's glow,
For beneath their leaves, they steal the show.
In this tangled tale of joy and mirth,
Resides the comedy of our precious Earth.

## Beneath the Surface of Solitude

In silence deep, the roots do speak,
With gossips that make the critters peek.
A lonely moss shared a funny line,
'Tis none of your business, this shade is mine!'

The rocks exchange glances of pure disdain,
While puddle frogs croak a humor strain.
A falling leaf, a whimsical flight,
Claimed it was training for 'leafy' heights.

Moles wear shades to hide their eyes,
Laughing at their under-earth disguise.
An acorn whispers, with seeds nearby,
'You think you grow tall? I'm just too spry!'

In solitude's grip, they find such glee,
Frolicking traits, a comical spree.
As roots grow deep, they find who's bold,
And playfully share the stories told.

## Echoes in the Subterranean

Deep below where shadows loom,
A party thrives within the gloom.
The dried leaves crackle, oh what a show,
As they dance with dust, twirling slow.

'Knock-knock!' chirps a playful sprout,
'There's someone lost, let's give a shout!'
But who knows where the voices dwell?
In echoes deep, it's hard to tell.

The energy flows, a thrilling buzz,
Ants debating who earns the fuzz.
A joke from a root, 'I'm growing older!'
'I'm still the best, just look at my folder!'

In this subterranean lark of cheer,
Nature's whispers grow strong and clear.
From fungi to stones, the laughter bleeds,
As life underground fulfills the needs.

## Chasing Shadows in the Soil

In the soil where shadows play,
They're chasing dreams that went astray.
A worm says, 'Hey, don't step on me!'
While laughing roots sway merrily.

The rocks get jealous of luscious greens,
While stinky truffles plot crazy schemes.
Together they dance, a funny parade,
Hoping no one finds them, hiding made.

Fungi whisper tales of the night,
With glimmers of humor, full of spite.
A distant squeak claims fame with flair,
As gophers plan how to get somewhere.

Each giggle echoes, an earthy affair,
In the growing depths, joy fills the air.
As shadows chase across the ground,
In the soil's heart, laughter is found.

## **Voices from the Loamy Abyss**

In the dirt where the worms reside,
Rubbing elbows, they laugh and glide.
"Hey, look here, is that a root?"
"No, just a shoe!" With laughter, they hoot.

Moles are telling ghostly tales,
Of carrots captured in leafy veils.
"I swear I saw a potato dance,"
Oh, down here, they take their chance.

Up above, a raindrop plops,
"Did you hear that?" As gossip stops.
The soil giggles as it shakes,
Nature's humor, just for kicks.

So join the fun in your backyard,
Where bodies wiggle, not so hard.
Let's dig into the silly bliss,
And share the laughs we surely miss.

## Shadows Where Life Finds Its Anchor.

Beneath the tree, the shadows play,
Glimmering sprites in disarray.
"Did you see that?" A squirrel shouts,
"Chasing leaves with wobbly routes!"

Earthworms gossiping in a ring,
"Did you try the mud? It's the new thing!"
"No, but I heard the toads were cool,"
And everybody plays the fool.

Gnarly roots twist like a dance,
Making friends in a rich expanse.
"Watch out for snails! They're gaining speed!"
And so the shadows gleefully lead.

In the land where the critters trot,
Life's a circus, believe it or not.
They gather 'round for a funny tale,
As the sun sets, they raise a scale.

## Shadows Beneath the Surface

In the underbrush where shadows bloom,
A frog declares, "This is my room!"
"But I thought it was mine!" A worm retorts,
With laughter ringing from leafy courts.

Beneath the roots, the quarrels begin,
"Shells don't count as furniture, Lynn!"
Turtles squabble; the sun peeks in,
While leaves dance wildly, letting the fun begin.

A gopher whispers, "Let's dig a plot,
Where pranks are brewed and laughs are hot."
They burrow deep for a golden prank,
Crawling back, chuckling, down the plank.

Giggling shadows start to fade,
As the sun tucks away, unafraid.
With tales of mischief, all is well,
In the earth's embrace, we cast our spell.

## Echoes of Entwined Journeys

In the tangle where the roots entwine,
A raccoon grins, "This spot is divine!"
Stories of acorns and nuts accrue,
While laughter ripples through morning dew.

The chipmunks chatter, "Let's race all day!
Through the thicket, hip-hip-hooray!"
But with their charm, they trip and fall,
And echo giggles bounce off the wall.

A beetle's boast of a shiny new ride,
Turns to laughter as friends chide.
"A snail's my racer; he's slow but slick,
He'll cross the line, just not too quick!"

So join this dance in the rooted shade,
Where each mishap is a joyful parade.
In journeys twisted, we find our glee,
Celebrating life beneath the tree.

## A Weave of the Verdant Heart

In a tangle of leaves, my friend does sway,
A tree with a joke that brightens the day.
Its roots tell tales of a party quite wild,
With worms as the dancers, all nature beguiled.

Laughter echoes through branches up high,
As squirrels in tuxedos share secrets nearby.
Each leaf a laugh, each twig a delight,
In this green, leafy fest, everything feels right.

## Breath of Earth

The stones giggle softly, they've stories to spin,
While mushrooms debate who's the thickest of skin.
A breeze winks at flowers, they blush all in pink,
Nature's a comedian, don't you think?

The grass whispers rumors, they tickle the trees,
As daisies gossip, blown gently by breeze.
With roots intertwined in a tangled ballet,
Life's little chuckles brighten each day.

## Heart of Being

A cactus jokes sharp, with a prickly punchline,
While daffodils chortle, their humor divine.
The sun winks down, it's a radiant jest,
In the garden's chaos, we're all guests.

Moss creates puns, growing thicker with glee,
As beetles share secrets, just you wait and see.
The essence of life laced with whimsy and cheer,
In every small moment, smiles linger near.

## The Hidden Stories of Entwined Life

Vines twist and tangle, a circus on show,
While critters below craft a whimsical flow.
A rabbit with wit hops near willow trees,
Sparks of laughter dance in the under-breeze.

Beneath burrows, whispers ignite with surprise,
Fish in small ponds share jokes with wide eyes.
Each creature a player in nature's grand play,
Telling stories of life in their own quirky way.

## The Memory of Old Trunks

Old trunks reminisce of the storms they outlast,
With knots and gnarls showing tales from the past.
They chuckle at squirrels who scurry and tease,
"Remember that time you fell short of the breeze?"

Branches recall love letters penned by the moon,
With shadows like secrets that dance to a tune.
Through laughter and whispers, they share their delight,
These memories tangled in soft morning light.

## Where Shadows Hold Their Wisdom

In corners where the shadows play,
The wisdom hides in disarray.
A plant once tall, now feels so small,
Its leaves are laughing, what a fall!

The sunbeam tickles, oh what fun!
While dirt debates, who's really won.
A dance of roots beneath the ground,
They spread out wide, but fun is found!

A gnome peeks out, with wobbly stance,
He joins the roots in silly dance.
"Why so serious?" he asks the air,
As laughter bubbles everywhere!

Beneath the soil, the chatter grows,
With every twist, a wise one knows.
The shadows giggle, they can't resist,
The funny business in the mist!

## The Language of Tumbling Stones


There once were stones that liked to roll,
They had their own hilarious goal.
Tumbling down the hills with glee,
Yelling jokes as they danced so free!

A pebble laughed, "I'm quite the catch!"
"Hey, don't roll too far, stay with the batch!"
They tossed and jostled, oh what a sight,
Who knew that rocks could bring delight?

With each tumble, a joke was shared,
The kind of humor that's never scared.
"Knock, knock!" yelled a stone with flair,
"Who's there?" rang out, echoing air!

They gathered 'round the ancient tree,
In their stony way, so carefree.
So next time you see stones on the ground,
Remember their giggles can be profound!

## Carvings in the Cellular Memory

Deep in the bark, where fun resides,
Carvings tell tales, with roots as guides.
A squirrel once sketched a nutty scene,
Where trees confided in branches green!

"Hey, did you hear?" whispered a vine,
"A story so juicy, it tastes like wine!"
The canopy echoed with hearty laughs,
As shadows flickered, like cheeky staffs.

Beneath the bark, the giggles grow,
Moss joins in, with a playful glow.
Lichens chime in with puns so slick,
Nature's comedy, a natural trick!

So carve your tales, let laughter ignite,
In every slice, a wink of light.
For in the wood, amidst our glee,
Life's funniest moments are bound to be!

## Musings of the Subgrade Soil

Below the ground, where the worms reside,
The soil chuckles, full of pride.
With every turn, the squishy bits,
They gather 'round for silly skits.

"Did you hear?" the compost said,
"I overheard a snail who fled!"
A laugh erupted, oh what a cheer,
The underground's stand-up always near.

The roots sent jokes from way up high,
"Why did the gardener say goodbye?"
"I don't know!" the soil went wide,
"To mulch he went, with worms as guides!"

With grains of humor, they sprinkle fun,
In every dark nook, where laughter's spun.
So when you walk on soil so rich,
Remember it's laughing, without a hitch!

## The Ground Beneath My Soles

I danced on soil, oh what a sight,
With worms as my partners, twirling right.
They squirmed and slurped, just like in jest,
We laughed as I tripped, oh what a mess!

The grass tickled toes, a feathery tease,
While rocks laughed aloud at my wobbly knees.
My shoes got stuck in the muck, what a plot,
A ballet in mud, oh, that's all I've got!

A mole raced me, I gave him a go,
He burrowed and chuckled, "You're too slow!"
Yet here on this ground, I'm the star, can't you see?
Even the daisies join in, dancing with glee!

With every fall, I just giggle and grin,
The earth's my stage, let the fun begin!
So let's stomp and leap, not care for the dirt,
For laughter flows free, wrapped up in my shirt!

## The Resilience of the Interred

Beneath layers of earth, where the lost do sleep,
They rise with a chuckle, not a single peep.
A carrot grins wide, "I'm taller than you!"
While potatoes plot mischief, as spuds often do!

The onions, they giggle with layers to spare,
As turnips tell stories of what's above air.
"Why squabble and fuss?" one radish did say,
"We're growing together, come laugh, hip-hip-hooray!"

As each sprout reported the tales of their day,
They showed how to thrive, in the strangest of ways.
Through muck and through mire, they uncover the truth,
That joy can be found, even buried in youth!

So when you next wander, beneath your own feet,
Remember the laughter, the roots that can greet.
For those who are interred, they plot and they play,
With humor akin to the sun's warm ray!

## While Roots Whisper Their Confession

In the dark of the earth, roots gather around,
Sharing tales of their travels, underground sound.
"Last week," whispered one, "I snagged a big shoe!
It tugged and it pulled, then I giggled—who knew?"

A sweet potato chuckled, "I burrowed so deep,
That the gophers took me for a nap! Oh what a leap!"
"While I was up here, I saw a fine bird,
Tried to dance with her, oh how absurd!"

"Longing to reach up, but stuck like a vine,
My buddy's a tulip, whose pot is divine."
The laughter erupted, a rootling affair,
As they weaved through stories without any care!

For nature's own humor, beneath all the grime,
Is found in the whispers of roots over time.
So next time you ponder, while standing so high,
Know that the roots giggle, they've got a good eye!

## Grounded Dreams in the Earth's Warmth

In the garden of dreams, oh what a play,
The daisies throw parties at the end of the day.
With buttercups buzzing, and bees doing tricks,
They waltz in the sunshine, all quicksilver flicks!

A crabapple tree brought a pie made of dew,
While snails did the limbo, oh what a view!
"Let's dream of the sky," the tulips declare,
With petals like giggles and joy in the air.

While below, roots were twisting, entwining in glee,
"Who needs to break free? We're just happy to be!"
They'd play peek-a-boo with earthworms so sly,
"Come join our fun dance, and we'll shoot for the sky!"

So as you embrace what the ground can do,
Remember those giggles just waiting for you.
With laughter and dreams, let the earth do its part,
For fun's all around, from the start to the heart!

## Gnarled Tales of Hidden Depths

In a garden where the weeds all dance,
A carrot once dreamed of a grand romance.
But every time it found a date,
It got pulled up - oh, such fate!

A turnip told jokes, quite a few,
While spinach whispered, "I'll stick like glue!"
Yet when the chef came with his knife,
They all pondered if this was their life.

Down below, the radishes sighed,
As silly potatoes claimed they could glide.
But in their muddiness, they did declare,
"We're the roots of laughter, so beware!"

So next time you see veggies in a stew,
Remember their stories and banter too.
For under the soil lies a world so grand,
Where gnarled tales await, just as planned.

## The Stillness Within the Thicket

In the thicket where squirrels play hide-and-seek,
A wise old owl gave advice unique.
"Stay still, young ones, when the wind starts to blow,
It's not just the branches that sway to and fro!"

A twigged-out rabbit shook its fluffy head,
"But what if it's gossip that fills me with dread?"
The owl winked, "Then just wear it like fur,
And hop through the thicket without a blur!"

When deer came by with a laugh and a snort,
They shared tales of thickets and wild squirrel sport.
"Life's but a jest in this leafy abode,
With shadows and whispers that lighten the load!"

And so the thicket buzzed with delight,
In stillness, they found joy, a humorous sight.
For nature's own jests spun all around,
In the quiet of thickets, laughter was found.

## Unseen Veins of Memory

Beneath the surface where laughter is sly,
Lie roots of stories that never say die.
An old shoe, a button, a can from the past,
A treasure of memories, molded to last.

A gnome in the garden declared with a grin,
"Each odd little relic has a tale within!"
So the stones in the pathway began to hum,
While worms crafted songs with a comical thrum.

Fencing with branches, the bushes gave cheer,
As daisies recounted their dreams of frontier.
For every bright bloom had a giggle beneath,
Enjoying the tales spun from roots and their sheath.

So visits to gardens bear gifts so profound,
With unseen veins where the laughter abounds.
Keep your ears open, and you'll hear them play,
The echoes of joy shaped from yesterday.

## **Growth in the Gloom**

In the shadows where sunlight dares not tread,
A mushroom grew sad, feeling underfed.
"I wish I could dance like the flowers so bright,
Instead, I sit here, alone in the night!"

A wise old rose laughed with a face full of thorns,
"Gloom's just a stage for the wisest of scorns!
Embrace your dark hue, give your spores a twirl,
And show them the fun that lies within a whirl!"

The daisies sneezed, causing quite the commotion,
While ferns flipped and flailed with wild devotion.
"Let's form a parade, with fungi in tow!
We'll celebrate gloom, make it a show!"

And thus in the dark, they crafted a light,
With laughter and joy bursting into the night.
So if in the shadows your spirit may sweep,
Just grow with a chuckle, and dreams will leap!

## The Bonds We Never See

In the garden, something's amiss,
With gnomes and fairies sharing a kiss.
They argue 'bout who has the best seat,
While worms wiggle nearby in defeat.

The daisies play hide-and-seek,
Trying to bloom, under a cheeky peak.
And though we can't see their tight-knit crew,
We can hear them giggle, through morning dew.

The ants form lines, as if to march,
And one trips over, silently arch.
A ladybug laughs at the blunder,
While butterflies flit for their grand thunder.

So raise your trowel, let's all toast,
To unseen friends we love the most.
In this tangled plot, we can always find,
The bonds we make, that tie us combined.

## Seasons of Interwoven Thoughts

Spring hops in with a giggle and cheer,
While winter grumbles, 'I'll be back next year!'
The summers are busy, with laughter and play,
But autumn just rolls on, in a sleepy sway.

In gardens, tomatoes might feel quite grand,
Until peppers gossip, about who's in demand.
And overhanging, a squirrel's debate,
On who'll get the last bite of the food on the plate.

But each season spins tales, of laughter and tears,
While we marvel at their unending years.
From blooms to the browning, a comedy show,
With nature's quirks, on the grandest tableau.

So sit back and relish this colorful dance,
Nature's own jesters, in a comical trance.
In every change, let joy meet the eye,
As life weaves its fabric, to the wind's lullaby.

## **Threads of Nature's Narrative**

In tangled roots, a story unfolds,
Of whispered secrets and laughter retold.
The grass sways low, and the flowers stand tall,
While squirrels plot mischief through every brawl.

There's chatter among the ladybugs bright,
Debating the shine of their polka-dot sight.
And bees hum away, like they're on a spree,
While ants cheerlead their mates with a tee-hee.

From branches above, a wise owl observes,
With a chuckle for leaves, and those twisty curves.
And when night falls, the stars start to wink,
While crickets compose a tune, what do you think?

So here's to the tales this nature contrives,
To the comic misfits that frolic and dive.
In every green nook, laughter intertwines,
Woven together, like mystical lines.

## **Silent Journeys in Silt**

In beds of silt, where the critters roam,
A tale of mischief blooms like foam.
The snails take their time, but the ants race ahead,
While the mushrooms gossip, over crumbs of bread.

A beetle in armor struts with a puff,
And ducks quack loudly, saying "That's tough!"
With each squishy step through their muddy domain,
They chase away woes like a runaway train.

Frogs play hopscotch on lily pad rings,
And sing of the joys that summer brings.
While visiting fish make ripples and squawks,
Exchanging their gags, while munching on rocks.

So here's to the journeys below our feet,
To giggles and grumbles in this watery seat.
In silence they venture, with tales to unfold,
In the silt where nature's funny stories are told.

www.ingramcontent.com/pod-product-compliance
Lightning Source LLC
Chambersburg PA
CBHW071429130526
44590CB00064B/2816